RHYTHM GUITAR

THE *Ranger Doug* WAY

With Suze Spencer Marshall

Layout by David Collins
Douglas Green Photo, Jim McGuire
Suze Marshall Photos, Lisa DiMarco of Northwest Photography

ISBN 978-1-57424-204-1
SAN-683-8022

Table of Contents:

Foreword. 5

Welcome. 6

A Little History. 8

A Little Rhythm Guitar Theory. 11

The Right Hand. 14

My Story. 16

My Guitars. 18

The Basic Chords 19

The Tunes. 20

After You've Gone. 26

Ain't Misbehavin'. 27

All Of Me. 28

Along The Navajo Trail. 29

Amber Eyes. 30

Avalon. 31

    Level 1. 31

    Level 2. 32

    Level 3. 33

Compadres In The Old Sierra Madre. . . . 34

Embraceable You. 35

How High The Moon. 36

Idaho. 37

Jesse's Polka (Jesusita). 38

Limehouse Blues. 40

Lullaby Of Birdland. 41

Miss Molly. 42

Oh Lady, Be Good. 43

Out Of Nowhere. 44

Polka Dots and Moonbeams. 45

Racing With The Moon. 46

Red River Valley. 47

Right Or Wrong. 48

Sally Goodin. 49

    Level 1. 49

    Level 2. 49

    Level 3. 50

    Level 4. 50

Suzette's Blues 51

Tangerine. 52

That's How The Yodel Was Born. . . 53

Tumbling Tumbleweeds. 55

    Level 1. 55

    Level 2. 56

Wah-Hoo. 57

(The) Yellow Rose Of Texas. 58

    Level 1. 58

    Level 2. 59

Thanks & Dedication

Thanks are due of course to Ron Middlebrook, who never failed to believe in this project and without whose enthusiasm it would never have come to be, and also to Joey Miskulin and Michael Pettersen for encouragement and help with untangling small but thorny little musical knots. Thanks also for my late uncles Hank Peterson and Arvid Peterson for introducing me to the guitar all those years ago. Profoundest thanks are due to my collaborator Suze Marshall for doing the hard, hard work; I could have never done it without her musical skills, organized mind, astonishing persistence, and unfailing good spirits. Along with the occasional bottle of Whidbey's Island Port.

Dedication:

To the boys and girls of the loosely knit but highly dedicated keepers of the swing rhythm guitar flame. I think John Parrott came up with the name Rhythm Thunder, and this book is dedicated to him and all the other rhythm thunderers who continually inspire me: Michael Pettersen, Jay Brodersen, Tony Marcus, Andy Reiss, Jerry Krahn, Jerry Compton, Don Stiernberg and my collaborator Suzette Spencer Marshall. And to Homer Haynes and Allen Reuss and especially Freddie Green, who defines Rhythm Thunder.

Douglas Green

Many thanks to Ron Middlebrook for his encouragement and enthusiasm, and for trusting that we'd actually finish the manuscripts in our lifetime. Thanks to Joey, Slim and Woody for being so gracious and patient with me hanging around with the ever present notepad. And, a mighty big thank you to my comrade Douglas Green, for inviting me to sit across from him and his magnificent Stromberg and place all these dots on chord frames. I've enjoyed every minute of the project, and thank him most sincerely for being so very patient and willing to play these progressions . . . over, and over, and over, that we all might learn and enjoy this music as much as he does.

Dedication:

To my late grandfather, John Spencer, who's love for guitar chords and rhythm playing sparked a lifetime of musical fire in me, and to fabulous and inspirational rhythm players of past, Karl Farr, Lloyd Perryman, Bennie Nawahi and Freddie Green. To Mike Dowling, Michael Dunn and Douglas Green, master keepers of the swing rhythm guitar flame today, and to Lauren Siess . . . who at eight years of age is an inspiration to all who hear her play.

Suze Spencer Marshall

Foreword

Suze Spencer Marshall . . as a child, I thought everyone played music. We didn't have TV and only turned the radio on for special programs. My grandparents, their extended family and friends were all musicians, and I loved their music. Grandpa's 78 records were worn out from hours of spinning on my little red Victrola as I played along. I enjoyed singing in choirs and ensembles in school, though not picking up the guitar much until my children were toddlers. A few years later, I went back to college to study music. My grandfather John Spencer, Karl Farr and Lloyd Perryman were my early guitar heroes, all fantastic rhythm guitarists. Later, Freddie Green's amazing rhythm guitar work inspired me, leading me to seek out other masters of rhythm guitar of which you will read about in this book.

My home is in the beautiful Northwest, where I teach music and perform, playing guitar, mandolin, and singing in old time and western groups. Our western swing big band, 'Way Out West' is where I hang my rhythm guitar hat and thrive in that magic pocket with the bass, while the fiddles and steel guitar play along. Life is good.

For more than 20 years, I've paid close attention to the way Douglas Green plays. In his own words, lay the very heart of his style; "I just play what sounds good at the time." He chooses just the right notes and color tones, connects them together up and down the fingerboard and then delivers them with the right hand pulse of a metronome. As the transcriber, with a strong theory background, I've had the opportunity to observe his style up close, with live replay and slow motion. He's a master of inversions and one note wonders. Theory masters may raise an eyebrow here and there, but the sound of his playing always wins in the end, to the pure delight of his listeners.

A few years ago, Ranger Doug and I were enjoying an afternoon of playing each other's archtops, when he asked me where I had learned to play. My answer was that I'd spent many hours on a bar stool with my face 12 inches from a TV screen rewinding 27 seconds of an ancient film clip of Freddie Green. I'll always remember the whole face grin that statement brought, and soon knew I had a friend for life. It's been the most wonderful of pleasures to sit across from Douglas Green and his fabulous Stromberg guitars, placing dots on finger charts for all of us rhythm mongers to savor. I've loved every minute of it and am honored to have been a part of bringing his style to print.

Listening to Douglas Green's rhythm guitar style is much like the experience of a very fine restaurant. Each note of a chord he chooses to play is like the finest of ingredients. Spices delicately flavor without overwhelming, over-filling or numbing the senses . . . always the most complementary to the musical experience. He is certainly among the finest rhythm guitar masters of all time. - *Suze Spencer Marshall*

Welcome

Welcome to the world of swing rhythm guitar! If you are new to the style, or interested in expanding what you know, then welcome to our unique world. It's a world often overlooked by the audience, but deeply appreciated by the other members of the band; almost essential. And yet the rhythm guitar is the most zen instrument of any group, whether large or small: if it is heard too much then you are playing too much. The old adage of the big bands was this: you should feel it, not hear it. The rhythm guitarist is the ultimate team player: you are in total support of the soloists and the singers.

That being said, those of us who inhabit this world find it endlessly challenging and fun. In our limited but essential role the palette of chord choices and positions seems endless, and the business of laying down that muscular, solid groove for the rest of the band is a joy. Whether big band or small, or whatever kind of music you make swing--big band swing, gypsy jazz, western swing, country swing, small band swing, or in my case cowboy music--you are the heartbeat of your band.

My approach concentrates on a fairly narrow area: the role of the acoustic rhythm guitar in primarily acoustic bands. As we will note, the acoustic rhythm guitar was a fundament in most of the big swing bands of the 1940s, throbbing plangently behind rows of brass and reed instruments, but in today's world most acoustic rhythm guitarists play in small bands of three to six or eight players. The style which I have been playing for 35 years (28 of them with Riders in the Sky) has evolved, but basically works beautifully not only with our four piece acoustic group, yet also with the jumping eleven piece Western Swing group The Time Jumpers, who graciously let me join their august organization, and even in a big band Count Basie type setting in which I recently recorded. This style works in a duet (think of Homer and Jethro) and in a 20 piece orchestra, and I hope you'll enjoy exploring it with me, because it will probably work well in your group too.

A final note in these words of welcome: it is not false modesty for me to admit to you that no matter how facile my rhythm playing may look to you from the audience, that I am a pretty average guitar player, and certainly don't have the great hands that make for brilliant soloists. I bring this up because I absolutely assure you that even if some of the exercises in this book seem difficult or daunting, all it takes is time to master them. I've come a long way (who would have ever dreamed I'd write an instructional book!) on modest talent and a lot of hard work. It was work that didn't seem hard because it has been, and remains, so much fun. Playing good rhythm guitar is accessible to any interested player who has a decent sense of time and the passion to work on it. I'm living proof.

Gretch Promotional Advertisment

"I don't try to play those big 'concert' chords. I play just a couple of notes, sometimes just one, but it sets the sound of the chord. When you try to play those big chords, it can make the whole band drag. "
   -Freddie Green

"The minute you start hitting six strings at one time, the band stops. "
   -Bucky Pizzarelli

A Little History

The birth of the recording industry brought jazz from Chicago and New Orleans to all of America around the time of World War One, and the Roaring Twenties became known as the jazz age. As jazz matured from Dixieland to swing, and as both microphones and recording techniques improved, a different rhythm sound was needed. There exists, between the deep drive of the bass and the upper reaches of the soloing reeds and horns (or fiddles in western, western swing, or country swing) a sonic range that is perfectly filled by a rhythm instrument which is also a string instrument, an instrument which provides a chordal tone as well as a rhythmic pulse. In the early days the banjo fit this role, but the meatier sound of the guitar became preferred as time went on.

Lloyd Loar's famously revolutionary work with Gibson mandolins in the 1920s was every bit as revolutionary with guitars, and his L-5 guitars quickly became the standard by which all others were to be judged, although it took nearly a decade for the guitar to fully replace the banjo in most pop bands. These guitars were built with carved arched tops, and were going for an entire different sound than the mellow, resonant, long-sustaining sound of good flat top guitar. The archtop guitar was built for projection, for percussiveness, for a sharp brilliant tone (people often call this "cutting") that could be heard above (or at least just below) the volume of the brass instruments. The ideal archtop guitar is loud without being clangy, even in tone across the range of the fingerboard, and strong in that midrange where the guitar can be heard among the other instruments. Gibson enlarged the L-5 to 17 inches across the lower bout in the 1930s, and supersized the archtop guitar with the introduction of the large (18") and powerful Super 400 in 1935. Many, perhaps most, of the best big band players of the swing era played Gibson L-5s or Super 400s. Within a few years Epiphone, led by it's huge and elegant Emperor model, was also commonly seen; their dramatic good looks and strong midrange sound made them a favorite. Around 1940 Charles Stromberg and his son Elmer, who had moved from making drums to banjos to guitars in the 1930s, began making what many (including me) consider to be the ultimate rhythm guitar led by the whopping 19" Master 400.

"L5"

"Super 400"

Although the Strombergs made relatively few guitars, many of the legendary names in jazz guitar played the DeLuxe, the Master 300, or Master 400, including Freddie Green, Fred Guy, Barry Galbraith, Laurendo Almeda, and in country music Harold Bradley and Homer Haynes. Stromberg's companion (and rival) at the high end were the gorgeous art-deco D'Angelico guitars built in New York.

In addition, the 1930s brought a small but exciting flurry of interest in hot jazz played on string instruments: in this country it was Eddie Lang (on his L-5 guitar) and Joe Venuti on violin; from overseas came the sparkling gypsy jazz of Django Rhinehart and Stephan Grapelli. Parenthetically these players had a huge influence of two young Texans, Hugh and Karl Farr, who brought this adventurous jazz edge to the beautiful, romantic, poetic western music of the Sons of the Pioneers when they joined them in the mid-1930s; hence the interaction of swing guitar to western music and, decades later, my own interest in this guitar style.

Karl Farr
Courtsey of Karl E. Farr

The Time Jumpers

The big bands are all but gone now as popular music has continued to evolve. The glorious Gibsons, Epiphones, Strombergs and D'Angelicos languished for a time for lack of players, but the folk revival of the 1960s spurred a whole new generation to created home made music, to research the musical sources and roots and traditions, and in doing so to rediscover swing rhythm guitar, whether in old blues or old jazz or jug bands or old country or old western swing. Swing guitar still lives and thrives, in the resurgence of swing bands, in the growing popularity of gypsy jazz groups (like Pearl Django and the Gypsy Hombres, to name but a couple), in the revival of western music, in the continued interest in Western Swing, in dozens of country swing bands around the country, and in the hot fiddle and guitar work of groups like the Hot Club of Cowtown.

The classic archtop guitars are being dusted off and played again, and several new builders are making outstanding new guitars in the tradition. It's a fun and fertile time to be a swing rhythm guitarist, creating history and keeping it alive at the same time.

Lloyd Perryman
Courtesy of Kathy Kirchner

Whit Smith's Hot Jazz Caravan

A Little Rhythm Guitar Theory

Before we get too much further, a couple of paragraphs on rhythm guitar theory are necessary, although in a sense this has already been covered. To reiterate your dual role in your band, regardless of size, is to provide the rhythmic pulse, in cooperation with the bass and drums if you have them. If you don't have a strong bass player this will seriously affect your playing, because you will have to play a great deal more on the bass end of the tonal spectrum. I have the luxury of playing with a great bass player, Too Slim (and Dennis Crouch in the Time Jumpers), so for the most part I am free to play rhythm in the midrange, where the guitar is best heard between the bass and the solo instruments (in our case the fiddle and the accordion). So in the chords which follow, although they contain three or four notes, the emphasis is on the 4th and 5th string; the listener is only going to hear the one or two notes on the A and/or D string; he or she will just "feel" the rest.

What? One and two and three note chords? What sort of madness is this? This is rhythm guitar madness, for those are the only notes you'll hear in a full band context. A duet-see my later comments on Homer and Jethro-is a different story, of course. The guitar has to be the whole band when you are the sole support of one or two instruments; in a larger band you are color and you are pulse.

Why not full six string chords? Because they are redundant and cluttered. Read what two of the greatest rhythm guitarists, Freddie Green and Bucky Pizzarelli said. (*See page 7*). If you play an old fashioned barred G chord, you are playing the G note in three different octaves, and the D note twice. This is a nice full sound for a solo performer, perhaps, but it is mushy and muddy in a band context, where the swing rhythm guitar always strives for a muscular punch (hopefully, a punch with some tone, more about which later). The three and four note chords (again, of which the listener may only clearly hear one or two strings) are economical, to the point, and stay out

of everybody else's way while you continue to keep time, steady as the ocean. There are a million beautiful jazz chords for the soloist, but the rhythm guitarist needs to keep it terse and concise in a band context.

Another beautiful thing about the three note chords is their versatility. You'll see when we get to the chord charts that, depending on where you are coming from or going to, these voicings can be any one of two or three different chords. A three note G6 is also a Cmaj7 or an Em with a G bass. A three note Gm6 position is a C7 under different circumstances, and a Gdim7 as well. Isn't that cool? You will learn about six new voicings, but you are also learning dozens of rhythm chords because each voicing works for so many chords! An added bonus is that once you realize this, intellectualize it, and begin to feel it, the possibilities begin unfolding like a lush flower in your mind. Several people who were fortunate enough to see Freddie Green play, my buddy John Parrott most notably, say that for all the musical complexity of the Basie

Bucky Pizzarelli

band, Green played no more than five or six voicings all night: he just knew where to put them, and of course he had that unfailing rhythm pulse.

Through the years I have found that sometimes, a la Freddie Green, less is more. Lots of chords don't make a great rhythm guitar player, choosing the right ones do. Movement behind the soloists is exciting and energizing to a point; too much and you become a distraction. The rhythm guitar player is not there to dazzle the audience; he/she is there to support those who do. What we try to do is dazzle the band!

Freddie Green

Of course dazzle is the wrong word here, meant to be ironic. We "dazzle" the band by providing the most solid groundwork we can, playing the best chords in the most pulsing time. Most of the audience may not appreciate it, and that's fine; it's been my experience that the musicians do, and that's where we get our ego strokes if we need them. Because the rhythm guitar has a simple and direct function in the band, it would seem that everyone's approach to the rhythm guitar would be much the same. Quite to the contrary, when I think of that close circle of friends of mine who are practitioners of the rhythm guitar--I'm thinking here of Jerry Compton, Andy Reiss, Craig Chambers, David Sebring, Justin

Thompson, John Parrott, Jay Brodersen, Michael Pettersen, and Suze Marshall (Andy, Justin, Michael and David are superb soloists as well)--I am astonished by how different their approaches are from mine and from each other. Every one feels very very different to play with, every one has a different release with the left hand and a different way of holding the pick and coaxing the tone out of the guitar with the right hand, and each one makes any given guitar sound unique. And we are not even talking here about chord choices! The moral here is that there is no truly right way; every player brings his strengths and weaknesses to his playing, every player touches his guitar in a different way.

And nothing points this out more clearly than listening closely to my rhythm guitar idols: Freddie Green and Henry "Homer" Haynes. Green was born in South Carolina in 1911, Haynes in Tennessee in 1920. Though Green probably had an influence on Haynes, they are close enough in ages that they were both learning and developing the art of the rhythm guitar at roughly the same time, from listening to many of the same sources. Yet their styles could hardly be more different: Freddie Green famously played a pulsing, muscular style in the Count Basie rhythm section which has been described as a combination of a Cadillac and a Mack truck.

Homer Haynes

His left hand was powerful, deliberate, and he compressed the three note rhythm voicings down to one or two notes, finding that small sonic range in the big band between the bass, piano, and horns. The tone from his Stromberg Master 300 (he also played an Epiphone and a Gretsch through the years) was similarly muscular, almost honking as he drove that D string above and through the entire orchestra. This is the definitive big band guitar style. Homer Haynes played in a duet, and had to BE the whole rhythm section; his constantly moving bass was jumpy and exciting, and he used much fuller chords; he played with a number of stops and accents; his tone (on a Stromberg DeLuxe , though also played Epiphones and Gibsons) was very rounded; he often made,(in my pal John Parrott's words), his guitar sound like a harp. Two very different, very wonderful approaches to the same instrument; the difference was the kind of bands they played in. The point is that your style will develop with the band you are in; Freddie and Homer would both be comfortable playing "Oh Lady, Be Good" but each would play it so very differently; you will too

A final word from my own experience: most bands play an eclectic mix of music, not swinging on every song. Surely Riders In The Sky doesn't. This style of guitar works great on "Wah-Hoo," or "That's How The Yodel Was Born" or "Amber Eyes," but would be, rather inappropriate on, say "Cowboy's Lament" (Streets of Laredo) or "The Arms of My Love." For these songs, I often switch to a good flat top guitar where the open strings, the long sustain, and the mellow tone have integrity with the piece of music being performed. When it's time to swing it is back to the archtop. Your own sense of propriety and taste will guide you with your own group.

It should be said as well that this chordal approach and this feel can be played effectively on a flat top as well, and often is. Many, nay most, of the gypsy swing players use the Maccaferri style flat tops Django Rhinehart preferred, and Emily Cantrell, of the popular duet The Cantrells, plays marvelous rhythm on a well worn Martin D-18. The point being that if you are just jumping into this style play it on whatever you have laying around, no need for a mad dash to Gruhn Guitars or Elderly Instruments for that perfect (and expensive!) vintage archtop.

The Cantrells, Al Cantrell (Al Ehlers), Emily Cantrell

THE RIGHT HAND

You can play all the fanciest chords in the world, but the heart of getting that sound out of your guitar is your right hand. Every guitarist has a unique way of holding the pick and striking the strings, and I urge you to experiment to find the way that's best for you. Find your guitar's sweet spot, the place where the tone just seems to jump. Experiment with gauges of picks (I like mine pretty heavy; many rhythm players like a very heavy pick), and the angle at which you attack the strings. You'll be amazed how different you can make your guitar sound.

My approach to right hand playing is a very compact stroke, 90% wrist and only 10% arm. It doesn't look exciting but it sure gets the job done for me. Think of the way Tony Gwynn hit a baseball. Again this is an individual preference: I happened to see a Duke Ellington short on the American Movie Classics network: his guitarist (obviously a recovering banjoist--he played a tenor guitar; may have been Fred Guy) used such a broad stroke he looked like a mini windmill! Use whatever works for you, but what works for me is a compact, powerful stroke. The advantages are more accuracy and more speed (when you need it; I'm not a fan of speed for it's own sake); in other words, efficiency.

Which brings me to another point. If less is more with the left hand, it is also true for the right: if you find that sweet spot on your guitar you don't need to bang it or thrash it to get the sound out. It helps to have a good guitar, of course, and it's true I'm spoiled, but the

Fred Guy, playing banjo, next to the bass player with the Duke Ellington Band

right stroke at the right spot on the guitar will give you all the power you ever need, especially in a small band setting where too much volume from the rhythm guitar can be distracting to the soloists and audience. This is much of the secret of Freddie Green's unique and clear tone: it wasn't so much the guitar as the guitarist. He knew how to get that tone out of any good guitar, and much of it was in the right hand.

Another right hand technique for swing rhythm guitar is very important: the way you play the beat. Most guitarists who began learning the guitar as a folk instrument are unconsciously wedded to the notion of bass-strum-bass-strum etc. This is not how we play the swing rhythm guitar. Often I emphasize the strum on the one and three beats, which establishes the chord for the lead player; a shorter snap, almost like a drum brush, comes on the two and four beats to keep the rhythm pulse. It's almost backwards to the way we learned folk guitar. To return to the master, Freddie Green, he and many of his big band contemporaries simply played four even beats to the bar, perhaps with a small stress on the two and four beats. A lot of these songs work perfectly playing strum-strum-strum-strum, four to the bar. I've found this works especially well when you go to an instrumental break if you've been playing "in two" (ie strum-chunk-strum-chunk) during the singing, it lifts the band into a whole new gear if you and the bass player play "in four" (chunk-chunk-chunk-

Freddie Green with the Count Basie Band, 1938

chunk) during the instrumental breaks. You hear this in western swing frequently.

Speaking of western swing, this four to the bar style of swing rhythm guitar works very well in this style, although the classic sound of this style features a strong bass-strum emphasis, punctuated by stirring bass runs, thanks to the great Eldon Shamblin, the guitarist with Bob Wills and his Texas Playboys. This emphasis was due to two things: Shamblin wanted more bass power than he was getting from Wills' bassist, and he had an electric guitar to give him the volume to play bass, rhythm, and lead. That is the classic sound of western swing, but acoustic rhythm swing guitar can be (with the proper microphone placement) a warm and welcome addition to a western swing group, and can free the lead guitarist to play solo lines while the acoustic guitar takes care of the rhythm.

Which is a long way of saying that if you started in folk or country or bluegrass music, your right hand may have to do a little profound relearning of old habits and mental/musical assumptions. But it's all well worth it that magic day when you are chunking along and suddenly realize you've made your guitar sound like Freddie Green's, even for a moment. That's the day you become a real swing guitarist.

One thing I can't teach you in words is the release of your left hand. The length of time it takes you to release, to deaden, those strings is a big part of your feel. That is something you can only learn by experience, and each player develops his or her own feel. In general, too quick a release leads to a jerky rhythm, while too long a release makes the tune drag. Again, Freddie Green was the master, and when in doubt refer to him! This is a vital part of your sound, so spend a good bit of time paying attention to it.

MY STORY

This is an instruction book, not an autobiography, so I'll keep this short. Two of my uncles (Arvid and Hank) played guitar, and I started banging around on Hank's old Montgomery Ward guitar when I was about 11, roughly 1957; could have been 1958. Like a lot of other kids my age I really got interested in guitar in high school thanks to the big folk scare of the 1960s. Folk led to old time country and bluegrass, and after I moved to Nashville in 1968 I met a couple of guys who played swing and swing chords and were kind enough to share their knowledge and expertise with me: David Sebring and Ron Hillis. I explored a lot of historical music in the 1970s and big band leader Louis Brown was also very instructive in educating me about how a rhythm guitar should sound in big and small jazz bands, which has been a set of knowledge which in some ways has been more useful than knowing new chord positions. By the time we began Riders in the Sky in 1977 I was playing swing rhythm guitar because it fit so well with the pulsing western beat of western music, and thanks to the unexpected (but very welcome) success of this little group of cowboys I have, much to my surprise, become nationally visible as a rhythm guitarist in an age where few of us are lucky enough to be spotlighted. A lot of friends and fans wonder how I do what I do on the guitar, and hence this book.

OTHER RESOURCES:

There are several valuable places to go for more on related rhythm guitar styles. A great place to start is with several other books. Probably the best is Charlton Johnson's *Swing & Big Band Guitar: Four-To-The-Bar Comping in the Style of Freddie Green* (Hal Leonard); an excellent primer though, despite the title, the examples are mostly played on electric guitar, which is not the focus of my style. Indispensable of course is Mickey Baker's *Complete Course in Jazz Guitar* (Lewis Music Publishing), which has long been the chord bible. It is difficult but worth the effort; however many of the advanced chords go beyond where the pure rhythm player wants to go, but the patterns and the theory are priceless. Dave Rubin's *Art Of The Shuffle For Guitar* (Hal Leonard) has good insights, as does *Swing Guitar Essentials* (Acoustic Guitar Magazine), and Joe Carr's *Western Swing Guitar Style* (Mel Bay) gives a lot of great insight into that unique style, though some of his chords are, in the words of my co-author Suze Marshall, carpal tunnel syndrome inducers! The traditional Texas fiddle backup and roots of Western Swing are closely related, but rather different, from what I play, but Joe lays it out clearly. If you want to get deeper into theory (every year I promise myself I'll do so!) Justin Thompson's *The Musical Alphabet* gives a very concise guitarists' view into the structure of music.

There are hundreds of recordings I could recommend, but I'll keep the list short. Freddie Green can be heard on many many Count Basie reissues (about the best I've found so far is "April in Paris" on Verve), but to closely study his style get the RCA reissue of his 1956 album *Mr. Rhythm,* his only full outing as a bandleader. He leads a fine soft-bop sextet (with Milt Hinton on bass) and during every Basie-style piano solo his guitar is extremely evident, and to rhythm guitar freaks really exciting. Nice shot of him holding his Stromberg Master 300 on the cover!. Not as interesting musically is *Rhythm Willie*, with Herb Ellis and Freddie Green on Blue Note, but still there is plenty of powerful rhythm guitar to be heard. If you bought this book to find out what sound I'm going for (basically, not exclusively), then these are the recordings to get. There is a good video on Basie in Ralph Gleason's "Jazz Masters" series, which shows a lot of Freddie (it's just Basie and the rhythm section) and a DVD called *Diane Schurr With the*

Count Basie Orchestra features several illuminating closeups of Green at work late in his career; just days before his death, in fact. You won't believe how high he had his action!

Speaking of my style, to this point my best work can be most clearly heard on *Riders In The Sky Present A Pair Of Kings,* Woody and Joeys effort on "Oh Boy," and on Riders In The Sky's recent 25th Anniversary album *Silver Jubilee* on Acoustic Disc. I do have an instructional video available from Too Slim's Mercantile (www.ridersinthesky.com), which is a good starting point, though my style has evolved and continues to evolve. It has recently been reissued by Centerstream in DVD format. There is no better place to go for Homer Haynes' clearest work than a Japanese BMG reissue of Homer & Jethro's two instrumental (non-comedy) albums *Playin' It Straight* and *It Ain't Necessarily Square,* although Homer's marvelous work is sometimes a bit obscured by a tastefully played but too loudly mixed snare drum. Gene Monbeck's strong rhythm guitar work is often evident on *Hard Life Blues,* a Soundies reissue of transcriptions by Roy Lanham and the Whippoorwills. And John Parrott's supple rhythm playing is shown to great advantage on *The Swing Sessions* (Cronyn Records). There is a good bit of Bucky Pizzarelli's work out there; it is well worth looking for. Where you can find Allen Reuss is hit and miss but his playing makes it well worth the search--some of the best I've heard is several cuts on a Coleman Hawkins CD called *The Hollywood Sessions.* Some of these recordings may be a little hard to track down but you could spend a lifetime learning from what you hear from these masters on these discs.

And for the computer literate it will come as no surprise that there is rhythm guitar on the internet. Try **www.freddiegreen.org** for an indepth information of the master's life and guitar style, with many fine photographs. This link is absolutely essential to the rhythm guitarist-- don't miss it!

A link at that site will then lead you to **http://personal.nbnet.nb.ca/verdell/JazzRhythmGtr.htm,** which is a rather complicated address for a fine site dealing with, you guessed it, three-note chords for rhythm guitarists.

Allan Reuss laying down the chords in 1938

Allan Reuss
Photo courtsey of Alan Rowland and the family of Allan Reuss

MY GUITARS

Our intrepid editor felt that you, the obliging reader, would be interested in the guitars I have played and play. Like a lot of guitarists I have been through many many fine instruments in my long career, and have a collection which is larger than my room to store it comfortably. But I'll hit a few highlights on the way.

When we started Riders in the Sky I was already playing a less advanced version of the style I play now, and had an outstanding 1939 Gibson L-5 cutaway, which was stolen in 1988. If you run across #96514 please let me know...I'd love dearly to have this guitar back and there is a small reward in addition to my eternal gratitude! This guitar is pictured on the cover of several of our albums, especially *The Cowboy Way* on MCA. Jim Triggs, while at Gibson, made me a beautiful blonde L-5 custom to replace my lamented stolen L-5; it is easily the prettiest and most beautifully made guitar that I own. It also graces the cover of several of our recordings, but a problem with continually warping pick guards explains why in some photos it has a dark pick guard, in some a white pick guard, and in some no pick guard at all.

When Jim went on his own and began building the Triggs guitar, he made me a big (18") cutaway beauty which in appearance, though not in bracing, resembled the legendary Stromberg guitar. I have played this magnificent guitar all over the world. He knew I had a fascination--well, perhaps obsession is a more honest term--with the Stromberg guitar, the relatively few master instruments made by hand in Boston from the mid-1930s through the mid-

1950s. These, to my ears, are the ultimate in swing rhythm guitars: they are warm, even, and project like crazy, partially due to Strombergs unique diagonal bracing system, and partly to the choice woods he used, and partly to the way he carved the tops. They are famously reputed to be incredibly loud (to be heard above the horns of a big band) but my experience is that while they are indeed loud they are not clashy or brassy; rather, their tone is punchy yet very full; they sound as beautiful as solo instruments as they do chunking three note rhythm chords. I've passed up several for lack of money in the past, but began collecting them when I could (largely by trading!), beginning with a 1948 DeLux a few years ago; this is still my favorite recording guitar, incredibly warm, even, and powerful at the same time. On tape it is rich and full, yet percussive in its role as a pure rhythm guitar. I've since added several others the the collection, including a G-3 and the incredibly rare G-5 (both cutaways), a Master 300 exactly like Freddie Green's, a lovely blonde G-1 and a couple of Master 400s, one a cutaway, the last he made. All date from Stromberg's Golden Age: the post 1940 era where the diagonal single brace and the choice woods were used. In fact, I have managed to collect the entire set (a true collection, in the words of George Gruhn, not an accumulation): one of each model in the golden 1940-1955) era. I tend to rotate these on tours, so as to keep the sound of each fresh and lively. My favorite (an almost impossible choice) is the 1951 DeLuxe cutaway. Perfect size, incredible tone, great neck, looks like a million bucks. My dream guitar.

THE BASIC CHORDS

This is no chord encyclopedia, but following are the main set of chords I use. Yes, there aren't that many, because as I explained, many of these chord voicings can represent different chords depending on the musical context. We will use all of these later, so be prepared to return frequently to this page for reference.

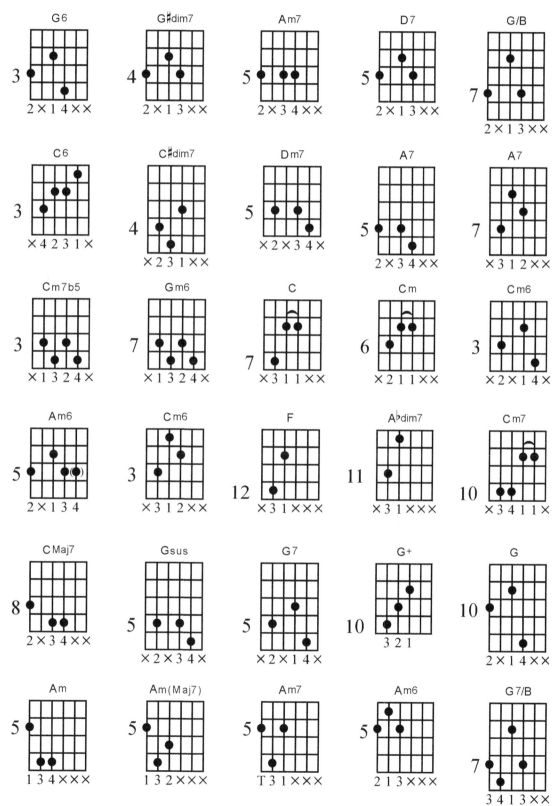

THE TUNES

The Tunes

Okay, let's, at long last, get into the tunes themselves. At the suggestion of our intrepid editor my colleague Suze Marshall and I have transcribed several tunes at two (in some cases three) different levels; that is, a basic rhythm approach to the tune for those of you who are newcomers to the style, and then a more adventurous and difficult approach. I rush to add here that none of these approaches are THE way to accompany a tune, merely a way, and a way that, for me, might change from week to week if not moment to moment. Each set of chord changes is not the way I might play them the next time (as Suze can tell you, to her never-ending frustration); they are merely a guide, and as noted Freddie Green and Homer Haynes and Allen Reuss and even Suze would play them very differently.

Another note on the songs chosen: I deliberately tried to pick tunes from the Western genre that many Riders in the Sky fans would enjoy playing, but since we hope this instructional will be enjoyed by a wide variety of folk guitarists who want to learn the style, or swing guitarists who are interested in my approach, I have also included tunes from the western swing canon, a couple of fiddle tunes, a polka, some jazz standards which crop up at any jam session, a ballad or two and some others I included simply because the chord changes are so cool and so illustrative of the subtle elegantly simple beauty of the rhythm swing guitar.

It will not take long to notice there are neither lyrics nor music included, which I frankly admit would have made following along a little easier. However, licensing more than two dozen tunes for a book like this would have made it prohibitively expensive, so all I offer here are suggested chord patterns to these familiar songs. If a song is unfamiliar to you and intrigues you, or if you've forgotten how all or part of it goes (I myself have to stay constantly refreshed or I forget), then by all means buy a CD and make the recording artist, record label, and songwriter happy!

SUZETTE'S BLUES version 1

Following one of those moments of transcription frustration ("Wait a minute! You did something completely different 30 seconds ago!") I decided to dedicate our first lesson to my collaborator Suze Marshall. It is a straightforward 12 bar blues on which so much swing music is based, and is offered in a very simple version and a more challenging version. This is a great place to start, because it gets you familiar with the three note Bb6 chord we will be seeing so much of, as well as the three note Eb7 and F7. Those of you just starting swing should practice those chord positions over and over.

SUZETTE'S BLUES version 2

Now for more texture: this is how I might accompany a blues on any given night; the choice of chord forms is practically unlimited, and how you will move from one chord to the next, what substitutions you will use, is very much your choice. Get used to hearing some of these substitutions for example, (the Cm7 to F7 for example instead of the simple F7) because they will occur over and over in every key and virtually every song.

SALLY GOODIN   version 1

One thing a rhythm guitarist is certain to do in the course of a long career is back up a fiddle player. And if you do you are almost certain to have to play "Sally Goodin." A lot. So here are three versions, at increasingly complex levels, to keep yourself endlessly entertained through a melody which only really calls for two chords. Those strictly interested in swing can skip this exercise, but it's useful indeed for the folk/country/bluegrass musician to have an array of musical tools to adapt to any situation, from a swing band to a fiddle band. Plus for those of you new to this style it's just a great exercise for your fingers and for your ears. This first version is as plain as it gets.

Now we start moving around a little bit, and it gets kind of fun. It's probably wise to note here that "Texas style" or competition style fiddling has it's own rather rigidly defined guitar backup style, and this is not that (Joe Carr's book is good on that style). This is more or less how I would play it, for better or for worse.

SALLY GOODIN   version 3

Now say this tune has gone on for more than just a few minutes and you are looking to play something a little more challenging. This is how I would do it, with the cautionary note that while you may learn a lot playing this version out of this book, this might be entirely too much in a live music setting. I am trying to get you used to the slides, in-between notes, leading notes, and chord substitutions so this is really more of an exercise than a blueprint for how you would actually play it with a fiddler. Unless you can play this in perfect time you're going get the X-ray stare from the rest of the band. Again, with rhythm guitar less is often more. When you get a little facile with these chords it is easy to overplay. A word of advice: don't.

MISS MOLLY   version 1

Time to move over to the western swing arena, with this lively standard written by Cindy Walker for Bob Wills and revived later by Asleep At The Wheel, and played by every western swing band ever since. Again the first version is for learning the tune and the feel, getting used to switching from one chord to the next. If you made it through 'Sally Goodin" this will be a piece of cake.

MISS MOLLY   version 2

This is the way I might play it with the Riders (or the Time Jumpers, or anybody I'm jamming with) on any given evening. That Ab diminished as the second chord, descending from the G/B bass glides seamlessly with the fiddles, and is one of those lovely occasions when you start hearing how the rhythm guitar enhances and supports the whole band musically, as well as keeps time.

YELLOW ROSE OF TEXAS version 1

Time to head west and do some cowboy songs, beginning with this venerable favorite. Many of you may think of Mitch Miller's march-time hit from the 1950s, but cowboy musicians have been swinging this tune for years. It also starts us playing out of the Eb6 position on the middle four strings, a position I use a lot since so many of our tunes are in Eb.

YELLOW ROSE OF TEXAS   version 2

   This is the way I might play it, concentrating always on not getting too jumpy or nervous sounding, just swinging steadily.   That's the way western music lopes.

TUMBLING TUMBLEWEEDS   version 1

   Bob Nolan's timeless western classic has a lot of chords before we even begin thinking about substitutions, so this first exercise is the basic form, no tricks but a perfectly appropriate accompaniment to the song.

TUMBLING TUMBLEWEEDS   version 2

   It's easy to get too busy sounding so be careful, but this is the way Slim and I have worked it out through 28 years of playing this song, with all the little slides, leading notes, and substitutions.   Again, you'll doubtless have your own interpretation, but this is a pretty good place to start; at least you'll know where I am coming from.

AMBER EYES

   Nothing complicated here, just a good loping feel and a fine exercise in this style in the key of Eb. It will also introduce you to that little descending pattern (found in line 11, the third line of the chorus) we will use often.   It is from my solo album, Songs of the Sage, on Warner Western.   If you don't already have a copy you'll have to download it from iTunes or some other LEGAL music source on line; the album is now out of print.

ALONG THE NAVAJO TRAIL

   Ballad time again in Bb. This is an intriguing song structurally and chordally, takes a lot of work but is so much fun to play once you get the hang of it. Riders in the Sky recorded it on our Riders Go Commercial album on MCA (long out of print), and I did it again with the Time Jumpers on their Live from the Station Inn album.   The wonderful story about this song is that one of the writers was drafted and was in serving in England, unaware that the song had been recorded and filmed by Roy Rogers.   He took a young English lady to the movies one evening, and jumped up in the middle of the picture yelling "My song!   That's my song!"   The lady gently patted his arm and said "That's all right, Yank, you don't have to try to impress me...I like you anyway."

WAH-HOO

   Sticking with western songs for the moment, this old classic (written by Cliff Friend in the 1930s, recorded by Ray Whitley, Bill Boyd and his Cowboy Ramblers, and many others including Riders in the Sky) really has a fistful of chords.   If it sounds too busy you can certainly play it more simply, but it moves at such a frisky tempo it's fun to jump with the whole band while supporting at the same time. When you get through this you will be a swing rhythm player!

AVALON

Assuming that whether jamming or in a band you will be playing tunes other than strictly western or western swing, Suze and I have prepared chord charts for several venerable swing standards that are likely to show up where ever swing tunes are swapped. The first, Avalon, a hit for Al Jolson way back when, has been broken down into three levels again, the first simply the basic chords.

AVALON, version 2

Now we add the rotating climbing and descending chords which are very much a part of my style.

AVALON, version 3

Now we do it again, this time with the little slides and leading notes. This is where it gets fun!

AIN'T MISBEHAVIN"

Fats Waller's classic, and a jam session favorite. The ascension at the front is always fun, and the chords on the chorus may sound a little stark in 2 note chord style, but will sparkle in a small band setting.

OH LADY, BE GOOD

Another indispensable song to know if you hope to play with other swingsters. Again, that lovely descension in the third line of the chorus we seem to find over and over.

ALL OF ME

Willie Nelson did a lot to bring this song back a dozen years ago or so, but just about every girl singer I know likes to sing this tune, so it seemed like a smart move to include it, and in a key many women find comfortable.

If you are playing these tunes comfortably by now then you have my rhythm style figured out, and can go on to mix and match styles and approaches as you develop your own. Once again I must refer you to freddiegreen.org for invaluable information on various approaches to rhythm guitar, not just Mr. Green's.

However, as a big bonus, we thought it would be fun to chart out my approach to several other standards, some familiar, some not, some western, some not; just so you, the avid student, could have more fun tunes to work on. The list of possible songs is, of course, endless, but here are a few:

AFTER YOU'VE GONE

Riders In The Sky recorded this in an odd key, Eb, but I laid it out here where we do it in case you are trying to follow along with our recording, from the Always Drink Upstream From The Herd album on Rounder. I worked long and hard to find the right voicings for these chords, always trying to stay in that sonic range above the bass and below the solo instruments.

COMPADRES IN THE OLD SIERRA MADRES

This classic of Woody Paul's gives us the opportunity to play in a minor key, which give us a few more chords to work with and develop, plus its interesting chord progression helps develop the ear.

EMBRACEABLE YOU

A pop chestnut and a beautiful ballad to boot. Carolyn Martin does a magnificent job singing this with The Time Jumpers, and our brilliant producer and accordionist Joey Miskulin (yes, the Cow Polka King) helped me devise some lovely and sophisticated chords. Pay special attention to keeping time on ballads; it's easy to let it slip away if you're concentrating too hard on the chords. Well, it is for me anyway.

HOW HIGH THE MOON

Another one you'll be playing with other swingsters. This one also took me a lot of time and a number of approaches before I was happy with the voicing. It's just my approach but it works in our quartet. For a completely different approach check out the freddiegreen.org website for a transcription of how Freddie played it: amazing how his mind worked, harmonically. His approach wouldn't work as well in a small group--a little too spare--but for Basie it was, of course, perfect. With this small example I urge you again to develop your own approach. But then again, you will anyway.

IDAHO

This is Suze's request, a lovely ballad Riders in the Sky recorded some years ago. It is one of the very, very few songs pitched to us cold ("Here's my tape, why don't you record one of my tunes?") which we have recorded. It was written by the late Frank Basso, a musician and songwriter from central Illinois, and has beautiful chord changes.

JESUSITA EN CHIHUAHUA ("JESSIE POLKA")

We thought it only fair to include a polka, since we've covered several other styles for the rhythm guitar. Same chords, same approach. This is a favorite among fiddlers north and south of the border, and if you play with fiddlers this tune will eventually come up. Woody and Joey recorded it in F, but we have it transcribed here in the key of G.

LIMEHOUSE BLUES

Another of Suze's suggestions, an old tune from the 1920s that many musicians know. Again, the Riders play it in a different key than many players do: G as opposed to the more common F, but learning it in any key will open pathways to others.

LULLABY OF BIRDLAND

Bebop classic, great fun to work out, chordwise. This one will keep you busy for a while!

OUT OF NOWHERE

Here's a tune where the swingsters and the Djangofiles find common ground, territory familiar to both. Pretty chords, nice easy tempo, room for the soloist to soar and the rhythm section to drive, but gently.

POLKA DOTS AND MOONBEAMS

This great popular classic is one of my favorites, particularly because of the beautiful way the chords desend from an F up the neck and glide right down to the low F. Figuring out how to do that is one of the great joys of playing rhythm guitar.

RACING WITH THE MOON

Well, okay, not too many people play Vaughn Monroe's theme song any more but if you run through it once or twice I think you'll find it has some sweet chord progressions. Interesting trivia: Bucky Pizzarelli was the rhythm guitarist in the Vaughn Monroe Orchestra.

RED RIVER VALLEY

Because this is such a familar melody it is a great way to start playing those rhythm chords up the neck, a good way to get used to them before the more complicated tunes come pouring in.

RIGHT OR WRONG

Another one for you western swingsters, a must-know classic from the genre, done by everyone who ever flirted with the style from Bob Wills' original on down.

TANGERINE

This one comes up infrequently in jam sessions; you can certainly play it with a Latin strum or in 4/4 like I do, or both. I just think the chords are great, though the lyrics are insubstantial fluff.

THAT'S HOW THE YODEL WAS BORN

Probably Riders In The Sky's most popular number through the years--at least before "Woody's Roundup!" --I just thought I'd show you how I do it.

In the style of

After You've Gone

In the style of

All Of Me

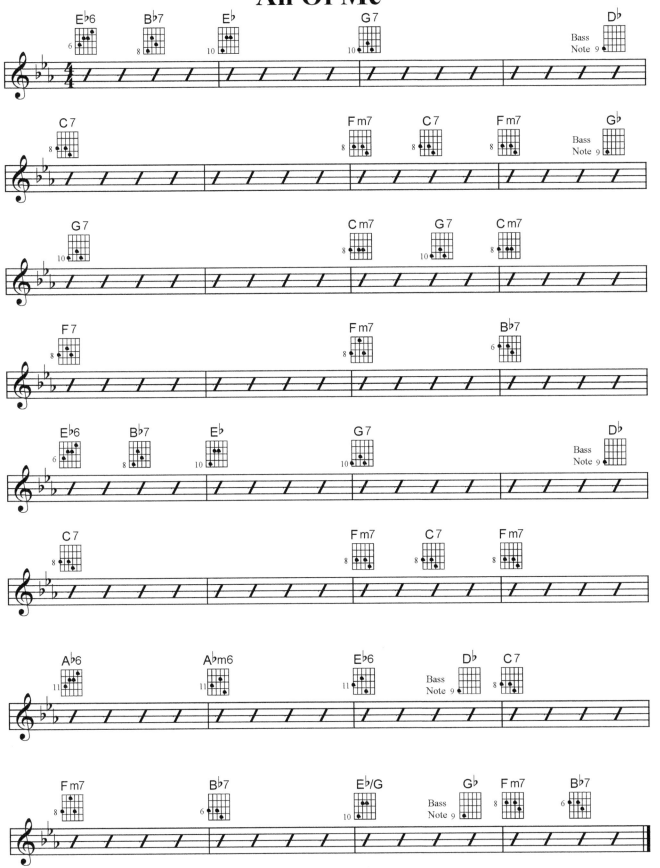

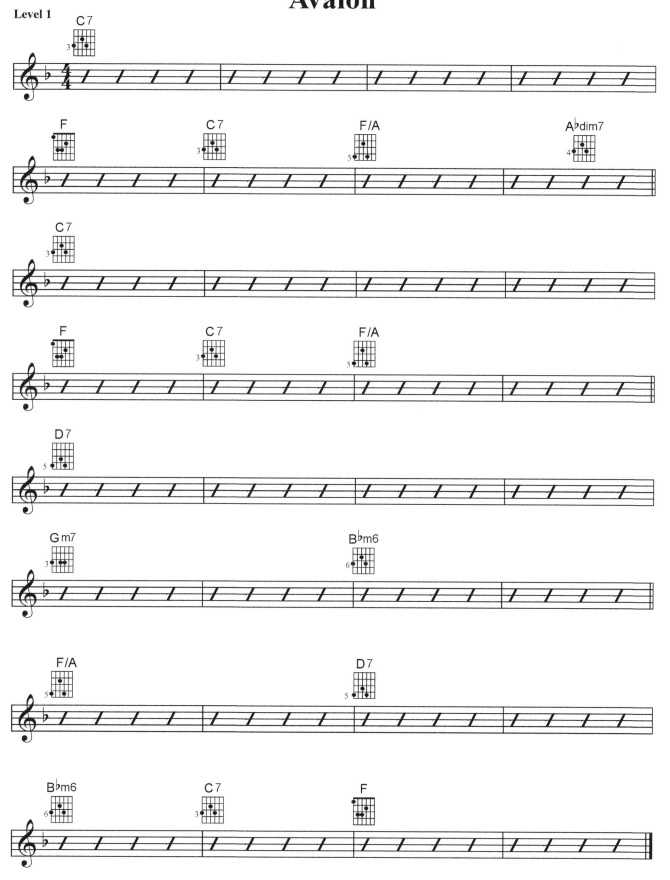

In the style of
Avalon

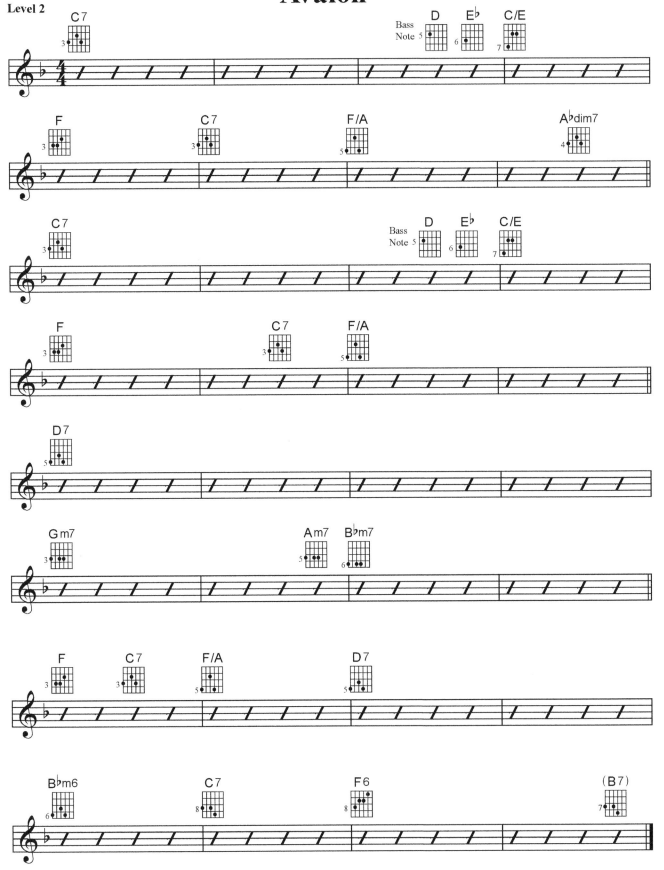

Avalon

Level 3

Compadres In The Old Sierra Madres

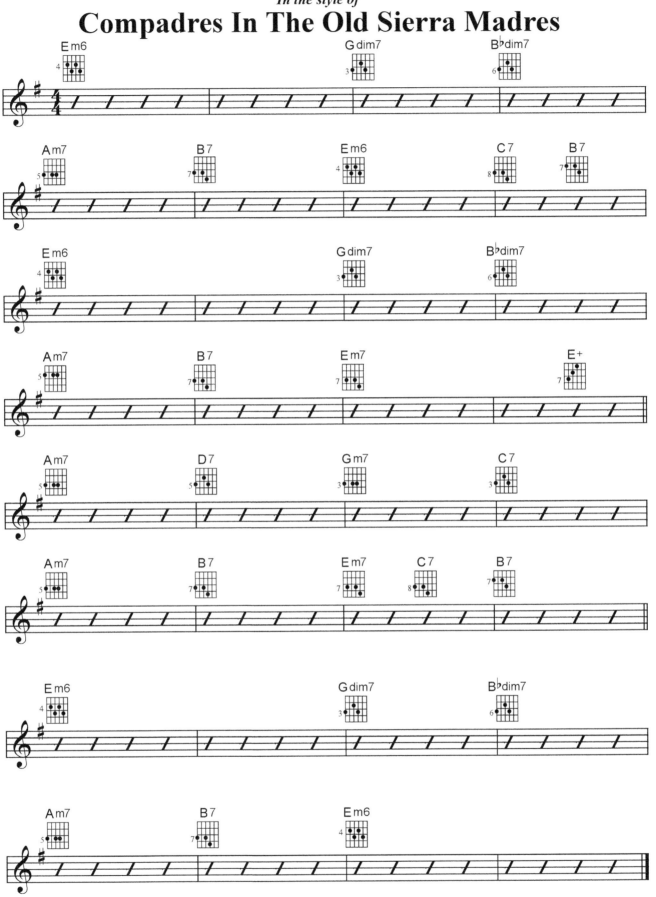

Embraceable You

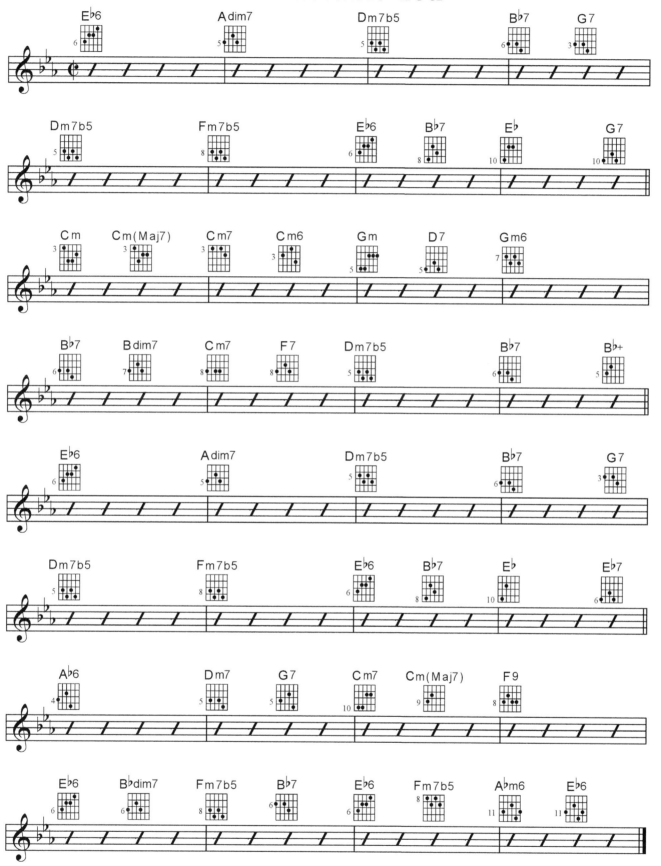

In the style of
How High The Moon

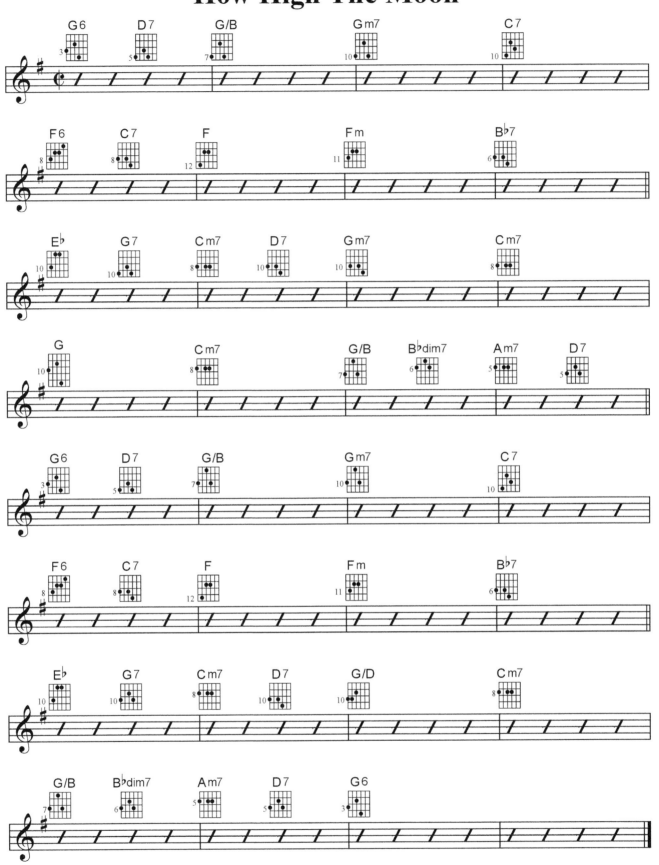

In the style of

Limehouse Blues

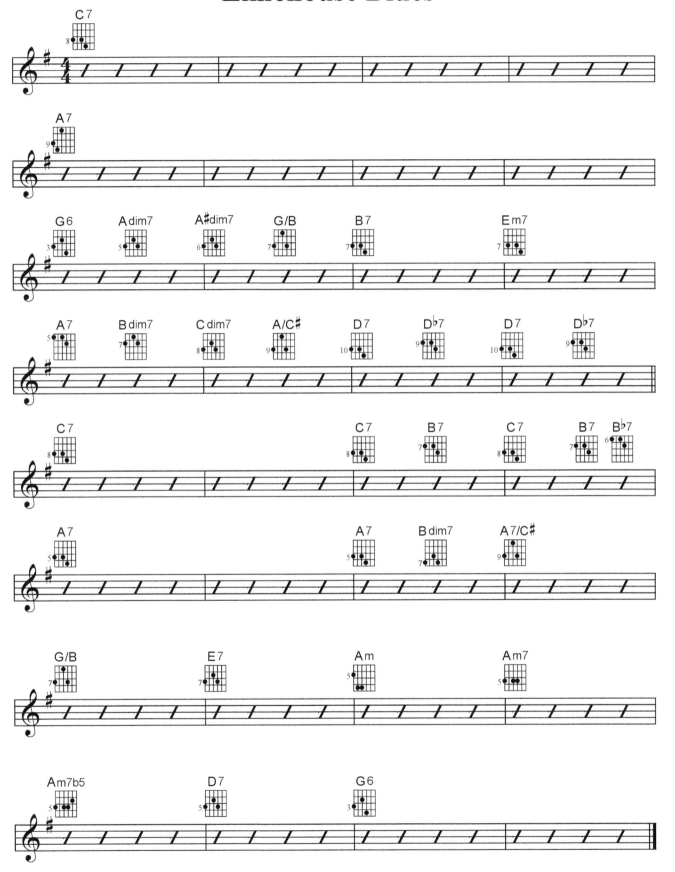

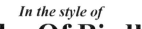

In the style of
Lullaby Of Birdland

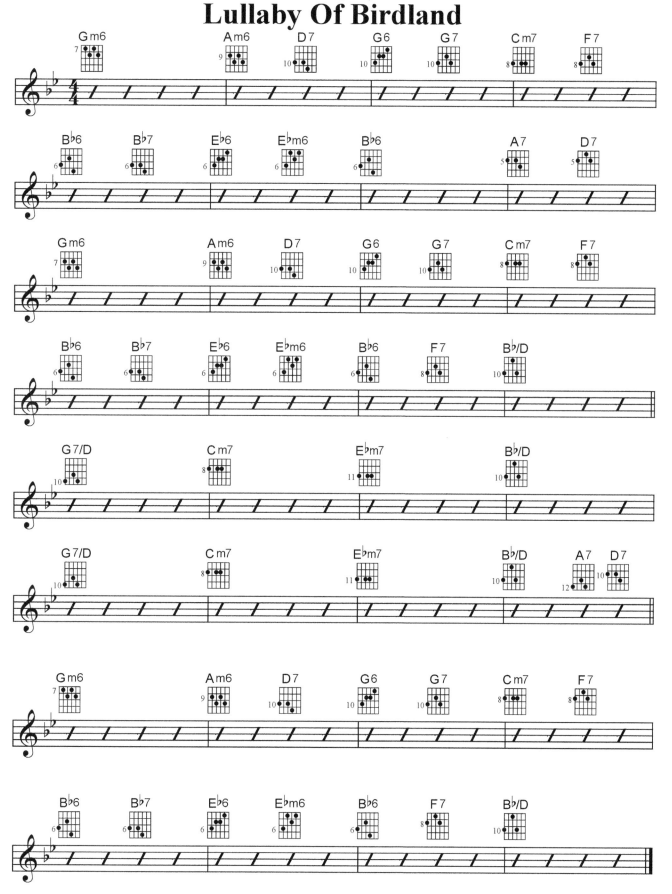

Oh Lady, Be Good

In the style of

Out Of Nowhere

In the style of
Polka Dots And Moonbeams

In the style of

Racing With The Moon

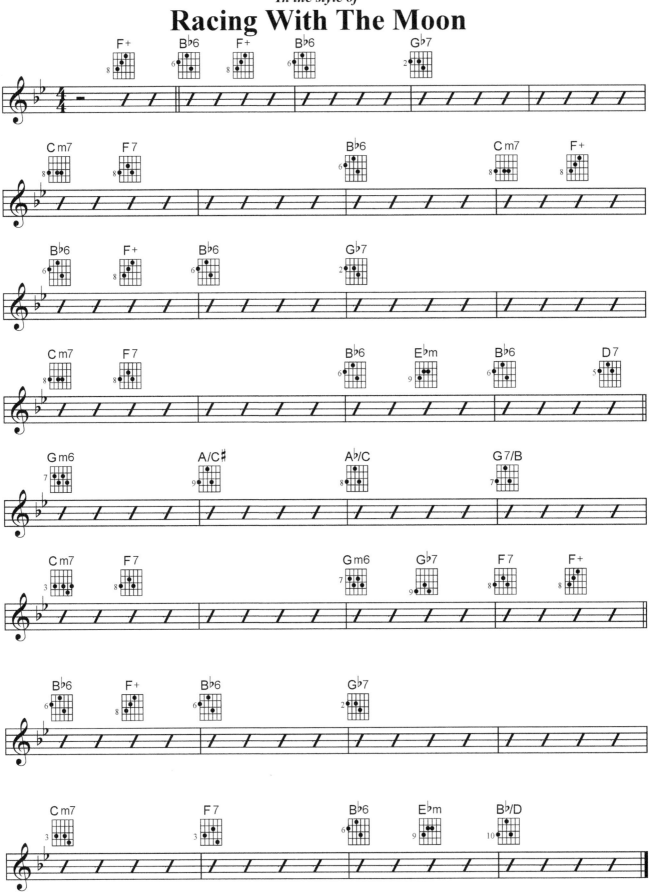

In the style of
Red River Valley

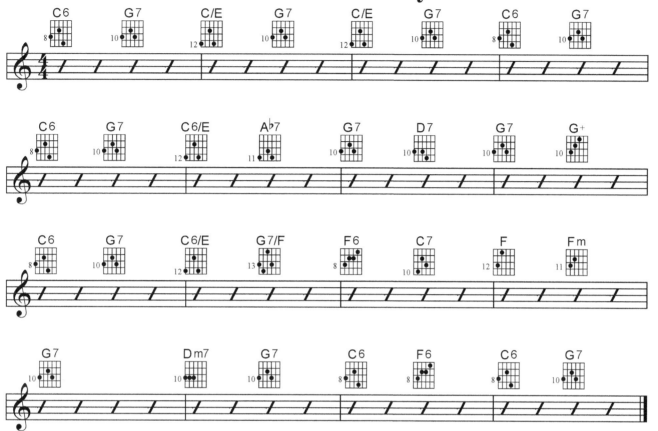

In the style of
Right Or Wrong

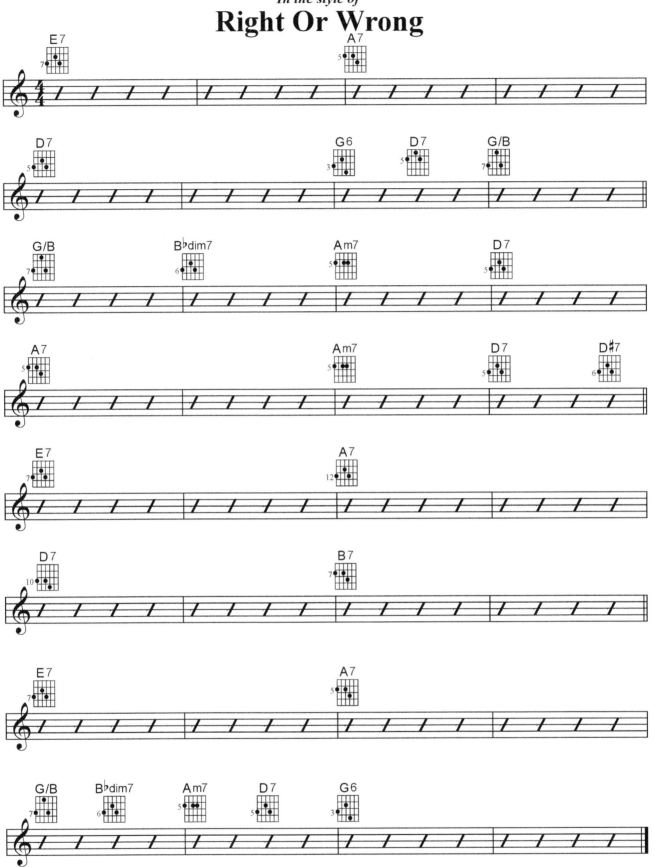

Sally Goodin'

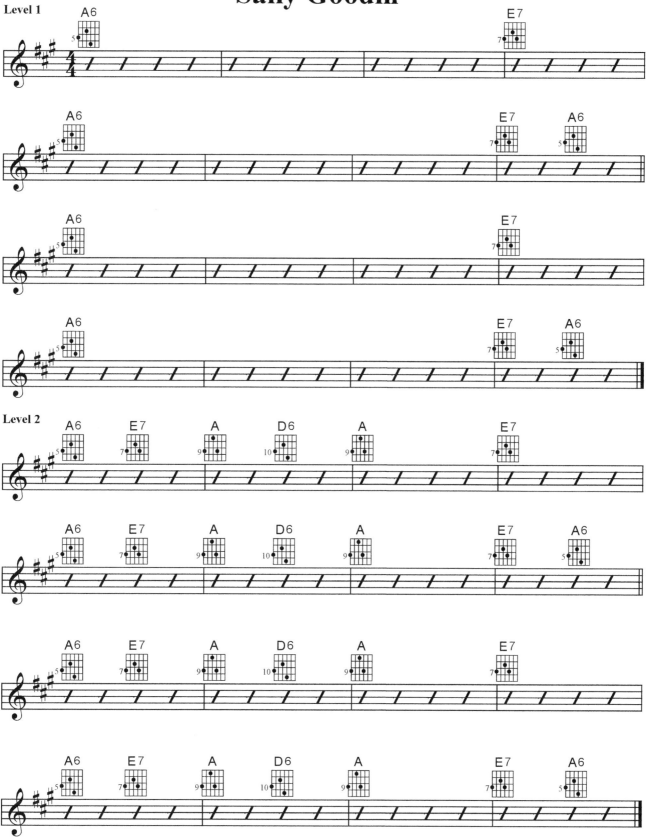

In the style of
Sally Goodin'

In the style of

Suzette's Blues

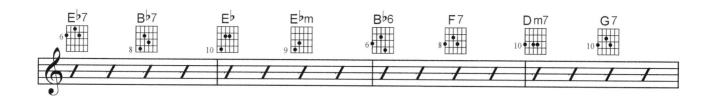

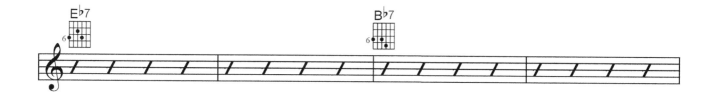

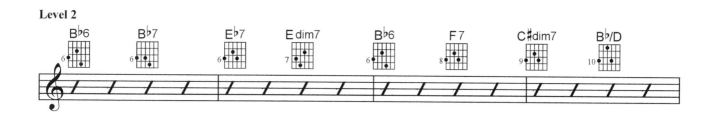

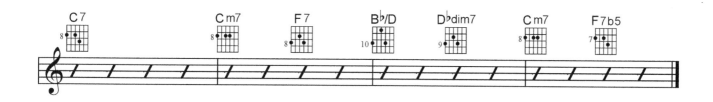

In the style of
Tangerine

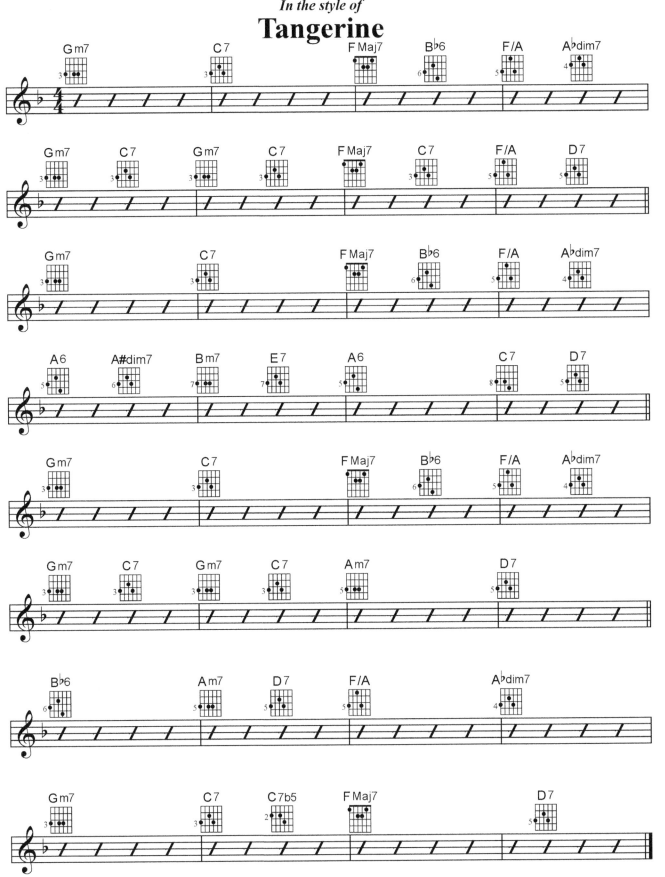

In the style of
That's How The Yodel Was Born

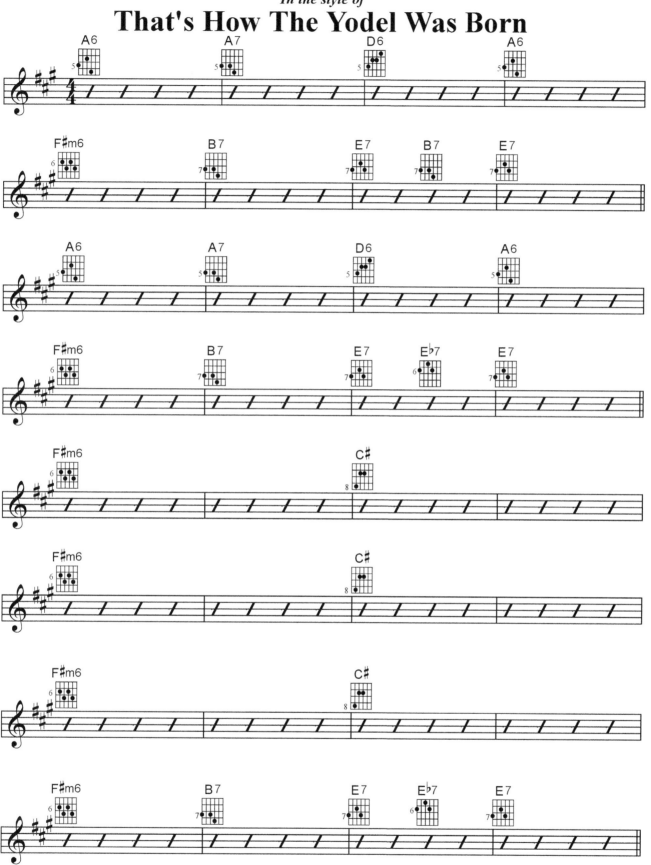

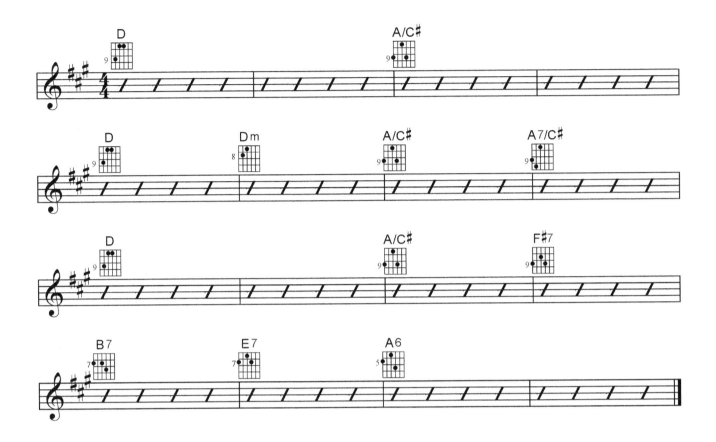

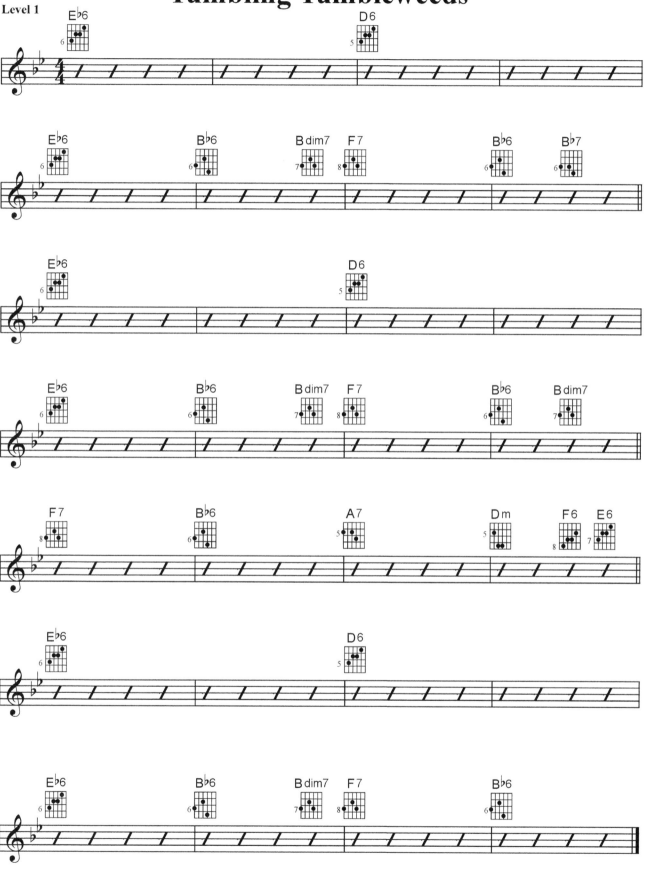

In the style of
Tumbling Tumbleweeds

In the style of
Wah-Hoo

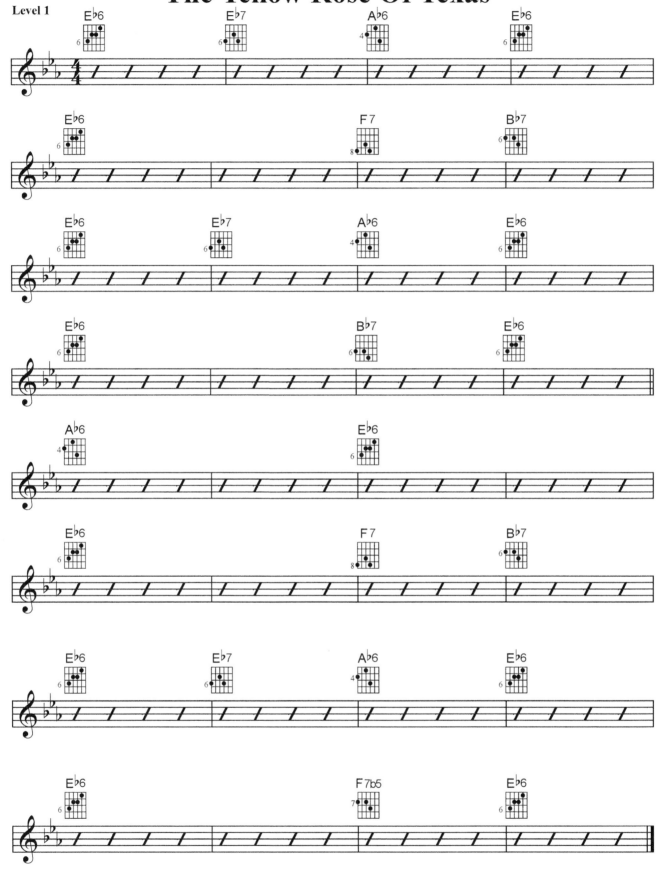

In the style of

The Yellow Rose Of Texas

Level 1

In the style of
The Yellow Rose Of Texas

ACOUSTIC BLUES GUITAR
by Kenny Sultan

This book/CD pack for intermediate-level players incorporates slide or bottleneck playing in both open and standard tunings. All songs are primarily fingerstyle with a monotone bass used for most.
00000157 Book/CD Pack $18.95
00000336 DVD $19.95

BLUES GUITAR
by Kenny Sultan

Through instructional text and actual songs, the author covers blues in five different keys and positions. Covers fingerstyle blues, specific techniques, open tuning, and bottleneck guitar. The CD includes all songs and examples, most played at slow speed and at regular tempo.
00000283 Book/CD Pack $17.95

BLUES GUITAR LEGENDS
by Kenny Sultan

This book/CD pack allows you to explore the styles of Lightnin' Hopkins, Blind Blake, Mississippi John Hurt, Blind Boy Fuller, and Big Bill Broonzy. Through Sultan's arrangements, you will learn how studying the masters can help you develop your own style.
00000181 Book/CD Pack $19.95
00000193 VHS Video $19.95

CHRISTMAS SOUTH OF THE BORDER
featuring the Red Hot Jalapeños with special guest The Cactus Brothers

Add heat to your holiday with these ten salsa-flavored arrangements of time-honored Christmas carols. With the accompanying CD, you can play your guitar along with The Cactus Brothers on: Jingle Bells • Deck the Halls • Silent Night • Joy to the World • What Child Is This? • and more. ¡Feliz Navidad!
00000319 Book/CD Pack $19.95

A CLASSICAL CHRISTMAS
by Ron Middlebrook

This book/CD pack features easy to advanced play-along arrangements of 23 top holiday tunes for classical/fingerstyle guitar. Includes: Birthday of a King • God Rest Ye, Merry Gentlemen • Good Christian Men, Rejoice • Jingle Bells • Joy to the World • O Holy Night • O Sanctissima • What Child Is This? (Greensleeves) • and more. The CD features a demo track for each song.
00000271 Book/CD Pack $15.95

ESSENTIAL BLUES GUITAR
by Dave Celentano

This handy guide to playing blues guitars emphasizes the essentials, such as: chord changes, scales, rhythms, turn arounds, phrasing, soloing and more. Includes lots of examples, plus 10 rhythm tracks for soloing and improvising.
00000237 Book/CD Pack $19.95

FINGERSTYLE GUITAR
by Ken Perlman

Teaches beginning or advanced guitarists how to master the basic musical skills of fingerpicking techniques needed to play folk, blues, fiddle tunes or ragtime on guitar.
00000081 Book Only $24.95
00000175 VHS Video $24.95

THE FLATPICKER'S GUIDE
by Dan Crary

This instruction/method book for flatpicking teaches how to play accompaniments, cross-picking, and how to play lick strums. Examples in the book are explained on the accompanying CD. The CD also allows the player to play along with the songs in the book.
00000231 Book/CD Pack $19.95

JAZZ GUITAR CHRISTMAS
by George Ports

Features fun and challenging arrangements of 13 Christmas favorites. Each song is arranged in both easy and intermediate chord melody style. Songs include: All Through the Night • Angels from the Realm of Glory • Away in a Manger • The Boar's Head Carol • The Coventry Carol • Deck the Hall • Jolly Old St. Nicholas • and more.
00000240 ....$9.95

JAZZ GUITAR SOLOS
by George Ports and Frank Sibley

Jazz horn players are some of the best improvisers ever. Now guitarists can learn their tricks! This book features 12 solos (progressing in difficulty) from jazz saxophonists and trumpeters transcribed in easy-to-read guitar tab. The CD features each solo played twice, at slow and regular tempo.
00000188 Book/CD Pack $19.95

THE NASTY BLUES
by Tom Ball

A celebration of crude and lewd songs by the best bluesmen and women in history, including Bo Carter, Bessie Smith, Irene Scruggs, Lil Johnson, Georgia White, Charlie Pickett, Lonnie Johnson, Ethel Waters, Dirty Red, and more. 30 songs in all, including: Sam, The Hot Dog Man • I Need a Little Sugar in My Bowl • Send Me a Man • Empty Bed Blues • One Hour Mama • and more.
00000049 ....$12.95

THE PATRIOTIC GUITARIST
arranged by Larry McCabe

This red, white and cool collection contains 22 all-American guitar solos for fingerpickers and flatpickers. Includes: America the Beautiful • The Battle Hymn of the Republic • The Marines' Hymn • The Star Spangled Banner • Yankee Doodle • and many more patriotic favorites. The accompanying CD includes demo tracks for all the tunes.
00000293 Book/CD Pack $19.95

PEDAL STEEL LICKS FOR GUITAR
by Forest Rodgers

Learn to play 30 popular pedal steel licks on the guitar. All examples are played three times on the accompanying CD. Also features tips for the best steel guitar sound reproduction, and steel guitar voiced chords.
00000183 Book/CD Pack..........................$16.95
00000348 DVD $19.95

ROCK AROUND THE CLASSICS
by Dave Celentano

This book/CD pack introduces guitarists of all levels to fresh and innovative ways of playing some of the most popular classical songs. The songs are in order from easiest to most challenging, and a lesson is included on each. Includes: Leyenda • Jesu, Joy of Man's Desiring • Prelude in C# Major • Toccata and Fugue in D Minor • Canon in D Major • more.
00000205 Book/CD Pack..........................$19.95

THE SOUND AND FEEL OF BLUES GUITAR
by John Tapella

This comprehensive blues book features information on rhythm patterns, fingerpicking patterns, double stops, licks in A, D, E, and G, and more. The accompanying CD features several compositions and all examples in the book.
00000092 Book/CD Pack $17.95

SURF GUITAR
by Dave Celentano

This totally tubular book/CD pack gives you all the tools to play convincing surf guitar, covering concepts, techniques, equipment and even surf slang! At the core of the book are six original surf songs by The Torquays. You can play along with these six tunes on the accompanying CD, and for each one, the book includes a transcription, lesson and analysis.
00000279 Book/CD Pack $22.95

THIS IS THE TIME – THE DILLARDS SONGBOOK COLLECTION

This songbook features classic songs from 40 great years of bluegrass by the Dillards. Contains many of their most requested songs, including those performed by The Darlins' on the *Andy Griffith Show*.
00000382 ....$19.95

VIRGINIA REELS
by Joseph Weidlich

This unique book/CD pack features basic fingerstyle guitar arrangements of 35 songs originally arranged for pianoforte in George Willig, Jr.'s book *Virginia Reels*, published in Baltimore in 1839. The accompanying CD features all of the songs recorded at medium tempo and played in their entirety, and the book includes helpful performance notes.
00000241 Book/CD Pack $17.95

Book's and DVD's from Centerstream Publishing
P.O Box 17878- Anaheim Hills, CA 92817
centerstrm@aol.com

GUITAR INSTRUCTION & TECHNIQUE

THE GUITAR CHORD SHAPES OF CHARLIE CHRISTIAN
Book/CD Pack
by Joe Weidlich

The concepts and fingerings in this book have been developed by analyzing the licks used by Charlie Christian. Chord shapes are moveable; thus one can play the riffs in virtually any key without difficulty by simply moving the shape, and fingerings used to play them, up or down the fingerboard. The author shows how the chord shapes – F, D and A – are formed, then can easily be modified to major, minor, dominant seventh and diminished seventh chord voicings. Analyzing licks frequently used by Charlie Christian, Joe has identified a series of what he calls tetrafragments, i.e., the core element of a lick. The identifiable "sound" of a particular lick is preserved regardless of how many notes are added on either side of it, e.g., pick-up notes or tag endings. Many examples are shown and played on the CD of how this basic concept was used by Charlie Christian to keep his solo lines moving forward. Weidlich also makes observations on the physical manner Charlie Christian used in playing jazz guitar, and how that approach contributed to his smooth, mostly down stroke, pick technique.
00000388 Guitar $19.95

GUITAR CHORDS PLUS
by Ron Middlebrook
A comprehensive study of normal and extended chords, tuning, keys, transposing, capo use, and more. Includes over 500 helpful photos and diagrams, a key to guitar symbols, and a glossary of guitar terms.
00000011 ....$11.95

GUITAR TRANSCRIBING – A COMPLETE GUIDE
by Dave Celentano
Learn that solo now! Don't wait for the music to come out – use this complete guide to writing down what you hear. Includes tips, advice, examples and exercises from easy to difficult. Your ear is the top priority, and you'll train it to listen more effectively to recognize intervals, chords, note values, counting rhythms and much more for an accurate transcription.
00000378 Book/CD Pack $19.95

GUITAR TUNING FOR THE COMPLETE MUSICAL IDIOT (FOR SMART PEOPLE TOO)
by Ron Middlebrook
A complete book on how to tune up. Contents include: Everything You Need to Know About Tuning; Intonation; Strings; 12-String Tuning; Picks; and much more.
00000002 ....$5.95

INTRODUCTION TO ROOTS GUITAR
by Doug Cox
This book/CD pack by Canada's premier guitar and Dobro® player introduces beginning to intermediate players to many of the basics of folk/roots guitar. Topics covered include: basic theory, tuning, reading tablature, right- and left-hand patterns, blues rhythms, Travis picking, frailing patterns, flatpicking, open tunings, slide and many more. CD includes 40 demonstration tracks.
00000262 Book/CD Pack $17.95
00000265 VHS Video $19.95

KILLER PENTATONICS FOR GUITAR
by Dave Celentano
Covers innovative and diverse ways of playing pentatonic scales in blues, rock and heavy metal. The licks and ideas in this book will give you a fresh approach to playing the pentatonic scale, hopefully inspiring you to reach for higher levels in your playing. The 37-minute companion CD features recorded examples.
00000285 Book/CD Pack $17.95

LEFT-HAND GUITAR CHORD CHART
by Ron Middlebrook
Printed on durable card stock, this "first-of-a-kind" guitar chord chart displays all forms of major and minor chords in two forms, beginner and advanced.
00000005 ....$2.95

MELODIC LINES FOR THE INTERMEDIATE GUITARIST
by Greg Cooper
This book/CD pack is essential for anyone interested in expanding melodic concepts on the guitar. Author Greg Cooper covers: picking exercises; major, minor, dominant and altered lines; blues and jazz turn-arounds; and more.
00000312 Book/CD Pack $19.95

MELODY CHORDS FOR GUITAR
by Allan Holdsworth
Influential fusion player Allan Holdsworth provides guitarists with a simplified method of learning chords, in diagram form, for playing accompaniments and for playing popular melodies in "chord-solo" style. Covers: major, minor, altered, dominant and diminished scale notes in chord form, with lots of helpful reference tables and diagrams.
00000222 ....$19.95

MODAL JAMS AND THEORY
by Dave Celentano
This book shows you how to play the modes, the theory behind mode construction, how to play any mode in any key, how to play the proper mode over a given chord progression, and how to write chord progressions for each of the seven modes. The CD includes two rhythm tracks and a short solo for each mode so guitarists can practice with a "real" band.
00000163 Book/CD Pack $17.95

MONSTER SCALES AND MODES
by Dave Celentano
This book is a complete compilation of scales, modes, exotic scales, and theory. It covers the most common and exotic scales, theory on how they're constructed, and practical applications. No prior music theory knowledge is necessary, since every section is broken down and explained very clearly.
00000140 ....$7.95

OLD-TIME COUNTRY GUITAR BACKUP BASICS
by Joseph Weidlich
This instructional book uses commercial recordings from 70 different "sides" from the 1920s and early 1930s as its basis to learn the principal guitar backup techniques commonly used in old-time country music. Topics covered include: boom-chick patterns • bass runs • uses of the pentatonic scale • rhythmic variations • minor chromatic nuances • the use of chromatic passing tones • licks based on chords or chord progressions • and more.
00000389 ....$15.95

OPEN GUITAR TUNINGS
by Ron Middlebrook
This booklet illustrates over 75 different tunings in easy-to-read diagrams. Includes tunings used by artists such as Chet Atkins, Michael Hedges, Jimmy Page, Joe Satriani and more for rock, blues, bluegrass, folk and country styles including open D (for slide guitar), Em, open C, modal tunings and many more.
00000130 ....$4.95

OPEN TUNINGS FOR GUITAR
by Dorian Michael
This book provides 14 folk songs in 9 tunings to help guitarists become comfortable with changing tunings. Songs are ordered so that changing from one tuning to another is logical and non-intrusive. Includes: Fisher Blues (DADGBE) • Fine Toast to Hewlett (DGDGBE) • George Barbazan (DGDGBD) • Amelia (DGDGCD) • Will the Circle Be Unbroken (DADF#AD) • more.
00000224 Book/CD Pack $19.95

ARRANGING FOR OPEN GUITAR TUNINGS
By Dorian Michael
This book/CD pack teaches intermediate-level guitarists how to choose an appropriate tuning for a song, develop an arrangement, and solve any problems that may arise while turning a melody into a guitar piece to play and enjoy.
00000313 Book/CD Pack $19.95

ROCK RHYTHM GUITAR
by Dave Celentano
This helpful book/CD pack cuts out all the confusing technical talk and just gives guitarists the essential tools to get them playing. With Celentano's tips, anyone can build a solid foundation of basic skills to play almost any rhythm guitar style. The exercises and examples are on the CD, in order of difficulty, so players can master new techniques, then move on to more challenging material.
00000274 Book/CD Pack $17.95

SCALES AND MODES IN THE BEGINNING
by Ron Middlebrook
The most comprehensive and complete scale book written especially for the guitar. Chapers include: Fretboard Visualization • Scale Terminology • Scales and Modes • and a Scale to Chord Guide.
00000010 ....$11.95

SLIDE GUITAR AND OPEN TUNINGS
by Doug Cox
Explores the basics of open tunings and slide guitar for the intermediate player, including licks, chords, songs and patterns. This is not just a repertoire book, but rather an approach for guitarists to jam with others, invent their own songs, and understand how to find their way around open tunings with and without a slide. The accompanying CD features 37 tracks.
00000243 Book/CD Pack $17.95

SPEED METAL
by Dave Celentano
In an attempt to teach the aspiring rock guitarist how to pick faster and play more melodically, Dave Celentano uses heavy metal neo-classical styles from Paganini and Bach to rock in this great book/CD pack. The book is structured to take the player through the examples in order of difficulty.
00000261 Book/CD Pack $17.95

25 WAYS TO IMPROVE YOUR SOLO GUITAR PLAYING
by Jay Marks
Keep your music fresh with the great ideas in this new book! Covers: chords, dynamics, harmonics, phrasing, intros & endings and more!
00000323 Book/CD Pack $19.95

Book's and DVD's from Centerstream Publishing
P.O Box 17878- Anaheim Hills, CA 92817
centerstrm@aol.com